THE PENTLAND WAY: A WALK WITH HISTORY

By Bob Paterson

"I am a part of all that I have met;
Yet all experience is an arch wherethrough
Gleams that untravelled world, whose margin fades
For ever and for ever when I move."

Ulysses (1842) by Alfred, Lord Tennyson

About the Author

Bob Paterson was introduced to the joys of walking in the Pentlands by his parents in the late 1940s. His career in the army took him away from Scotland but when he retired he renewed his love of walking, albeit, initially, in higher hills. Later, when Munros seemed to have become almost Himalayan he returned to his 'Hills of Home'. He believes that hills, like Shakespeare, reveal more the more you explore them. He can no longer scurry along the Pentland skyline but there is much more to the Pentlands than healthy exercise. Like all true love affairs there is always something new to discover, appreciate and admire.

THE PENTLAND WAY:
A WALK WITH HISTORY
by Bob Paterson

Conserving, Protecting & Enhancing

Friends of the Pentlands is a Scottish Charitable Incorporated
Organisation No: SC035514

All profits from the sale of this publication will be
used by the Friends for charitable purposes

Published by Friends of the Pentlands
Copyright © Friends of the Pentlands, 2015

ISBN 978 0 9934160 0 2

Printed by GMP Print Solutions, Loanhead

DEDICATION

This book is dedicated to the memory of the late Dr Robin Aitken, founding chairman of the Friends of the Pentlands. Robin's vision was to enhance responsible public access for the benefit of all and this publication is one small step in that continuing process.

Robin Aitken with 'Purdy' 2005

ACKNOWLEDGEMENTS

Many people have contributed, perhaps unwittingly, to this publication but I would especially like to thank John Stirling, formerly Chairman of The Friends of the Pentlands, whose idea it was to establish The Pentland Way. John has also been a great help in getting the book published.

Had Will Grant not published *The Call of the Pentlands* in 1927 this work would not have been possible. Similarly, I am indebted to Susan Falconer, formerly Senior Ranger of the Pentland Hill's Regional Park. Susan's book *The Pentland Hills: A Walker's Guide* has been a source of both information and inspiration.

I am grateful to Hamish Clark and Ian Combe for assistance with route finding, Alistair and Susan Cowan for keeping me right on upland sheep farming, Roger Oakes and Michael Jones for their local expertise of the West Linton and Carlops areas respectively and David Pritchard, John Surtees and David Syme for their comments on various drafts.

I am most grateful to the National Portrait Gallery, London, for permission to publish the image on page 79, to the Scottish National Portrait Gallery for permission to publish the images on pages 80, 81, 82 and 88 and to Midlothian Council Local and Family History Library for permission to publish the photographs on pages 50 and 71.

I would like to thank the following for allowing me use pictures: David Buchanan for page 89 (lower); Ian Combe for pages 76 (lower) and page 77; Barbara Darcy for page 61; Tony Dore for pages 3, 11 and 56; Mike Gill for page 17; Julian Hall for page 4; Peter Harnden for page 54; Malcolm Humphrey for page 10; Calum McRoberts for pages 66 and 90 (both); Victor Partridge for page 91; Dennis Smith page 12 (upper); Iain Gidney for page 12 (lower); John Stirling for pages iv, 3, 8, 19, 20, 25, 42 (lower) 55, 64 and 70; John Surtees for page 59 and rear cover; David Syme for page 52 and David Taylor for pages 1, 67, 71 and 74.

The author is most grateful to Andrew Thin who has kindly contributed the Foreword. Finally, the Trustees of the Friends of the Pentlands wish to thank the James Thin Trust for their kind donation towards the publication of this work.

FOREWORD

I was aware of the Pentlands long before I knew what or where they were. A mysterious place to which my father disappeared from time to time to visit the 'Kips'. Somewhere that my grandfather spoke of with wistful longing while he hobbled round the garden on his crutches. Source of the water coming out of our taps. The name gained an almost mystical significance in my young mind.

In time I came to know and love these hills for myself, and more recently my own children have explored their ridges and gazed down on the vistas that spread out before them. The Pentlands are one of our national treasures. They are part of what makes Edinburgh the unique capital city that it is, and they have enriched the lives of countless Scots for many generations.

But the Pentlands are not just a source of recreation and wonderment for urban escapees. They are also a place of work, and have been since time immemorial. My first experience of watching a collie working sheep was on the slopes of Carnethy. My early understanding of the work of gamekeepers was gained through a chance encounter on Black Hill. This is an area peppered with artefact, and a landscape that has been shaped by people over thousands of years. In writing this book – I hesitate to call it merely a 'guide' – the author has achieved something both unusual and welcome. He describes the historical context encountered along the 'Way' at a level of detail that will fascinate and intrigue, but he does so in a style that is highly accessible. There are nuggets to inspire the imagination on almost every page. Wanderings in the Pentlands, whether on foot or from an armchair, will never be quite the same again.

Andrew Thin
Chairman Scottish Natural Heritage 2006-2014
September 2015

LOCATION MAP

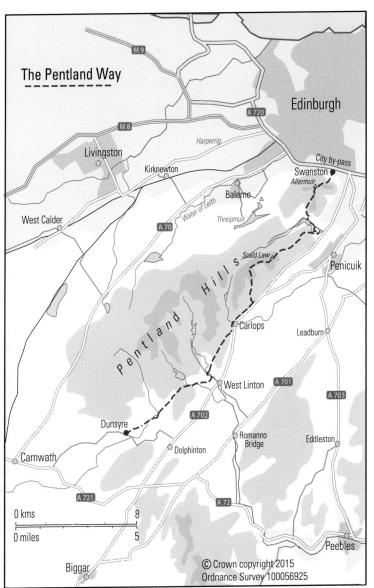

The Pentland Way

Edinburgh

M 9

M 8

A 720

City by-pass

Livingston

Harperrig

Swanston

Allermuir

Kirknewton

Balerno

Penicuik

West Calder

A 70

Water of Leith

Threipmuir

Scald Law

Pentland Hills

Carlops

Leadburn

West Linton

A 701

A 703

Dunsyre

A 702

Romanno Bridge

Eddleston

Carnwath

Dolphinton

A 721

A 72

Peebles

0 kms   8

0 miles   5

© Crown copyright 2015
Ordnance Survey 100056925

Biggar

NOTES

CONTENTS

INTRODUCTION

The Pentland Hills run south-west from Edinburgh for about 32 kilometres (20 miles). The northern hills are the most dramatic and provide spectacular views over the Lothians, the Forth and beyond. They are also the most visited area. The highest point is Scald Law at 579 metres. By comparison the south-west section of the range is much less hilly, more remote in character and much less visited. One of the charms of the range is that it provides considerable variety in a small, compact area close to Scotland's historic capital city.

Pentland Ridge from Allermuir

Essentially, the range consists of grass and heather-clad, rounded hills, although the Pentland ridge is higher and steeper, and offers a well-established path system. The hills are sparsely populated and most of the terrain is upland pasture. There are some trees around the periphery of the hills, some areas of forestry in the north-west and the northern hills contain several reservoirs which add variety to the scenery. The physical shape of the hills is essentially the result of glacial erosion and sculpting by meltwater. The geology of the hills is complex but, in general terms, the lower, rounded hills in the south west consist largely of old red sandstones and conglomerates while the well-defined northern peaks owe their formation to the presence of harder volcanic rocks.

The geology of the Pentland Hills is explained in an illustrated leaflet called *Pentland Rocks,* published by Lothian and Borders GeoConservation (www.edinburghgeolcoc.org) and is available from the Regional Park.

The Pentland Hills Regional Park was designated in 1986 and covers some 90 square kilometres of the northern Pentlands. The Park's Natural Heritage Service, formerly the Ranger Service, seeks to ensure the integration of responsible access with farming and other land usage. To find out more visit: www.pentlandhills.org

The concept of creating a Pentland Way was the idea of John Stirling, formerly Chairman of the Friends of the Pentlands. The idea was first discussed in 2012 and in 2014 the route was waymarked. From the beginning it was envisaged that some form of publication should be produced to publicise The Way and, more importantly, to show that there is an unseen story of the past behind everything that today's walker can see.

The Friends of the Pentlands held their initial meeting in March 2003. From that tentative beginning a small but vigorous organisation evolved which seeks to act as a catalyst to promote the conservation, protection and enhancement of the Pentland Hills with particular emphasis on recreational quality, public access, cultural heritage, landscape and biodiversity.

Harlaw Wildlife Garden

The Friends have an annual programme of walks and talks but, more importantly, they carry out a variety of projects in the hills with the support of land managers and the Natural Heritage Service. These include the construction of new paths, the maintenance of existing paths, tree planting, the development of a wildflower meadow, assistance with the maintenance of a wildlife garden and litter picking in 'black spots'. Currently the Friends spend more than 6,000 hours per annum to conserve, protect and enhance the Pentlands.

Larger projects, such as the erection of footbridges and bird hides, have been undertaken by contractors and paid for by grant funding. Find out more by visiting: www.pentlandfriends. org.uk

The Friends work closely with the Natural Heritage Service within the Regional Park, and greatly benefit from their advice and expertise, but the Friends' area of interest covers all of the Pentlands, not just the Regional Park.

The Friends have also been responsible for several publications and this book is the most recent of these initiatives. Although its central theme is a route through the hills it aims to be much more than a guide book. Indeed, it has aspirations to be as interesting to those who can no longer walk on hill paths as to those who thrive on them. This book seeks to bring to life much that may be invisible to the casual walker in the hope that it might bring a new dimension to their appreciation of the Pentlands.

Will Grant wrote of 'The Call of the Pentlands' nearly a century ago and I happily reiterate his message. "The more we tramp these breezy uplands, the more friendly they become; and the more we love them, the more they give to us: their call is unmistakable, and their appeal is as varied as the sky of an April day"[1].

The Call of the Pentlands

The Pentlands and their immediate surroundings have provided a home and a livelihood, albeit in many cases a hard one, for the last 5,000 years. There is evidence of the presence of ancient burial cairns, prehistoric farming communities, fortified settlements and hill forts, the Roman occupation, visits by early Scottish monarchs, battles involving Covenanters, raids

1   Grant, p14.

by Jacobites and tales involving witches. There is also a strong association with important literary figures. In short The Way is a journey immersed in the history of our cultural past.

Will Grant also recognised that the Pentlands were not just the province of walkers and, again, I share his sentiment. "The exercise of walking means fitness of body, mind and spirit to many whose interest in the hills is real and practical. But there are others for whom the exercise may not always be possible, but who delight to read about it, to think of the great walks they are going to take, and the hills they hope to climb, whose interest it may be is but sentimental. And there are those now far over-seas, whose love for the Pentland Hills is wrapped round their fondest thoughts of home. May all such, as they read this book, be able to catch something of the magic atmosphere they know and love, and feel the tang of the dewy moorland and the purple heather, and be revived by the fresh and bracing winds that blow from off these Hills of Happy Memories"[2].

Hills of Happy Memories

2   Grant p12-13

I urge you to respond to 'The Call of the Pentlands', there is something in these hills and their history for everyone. Walk The Way to enjoy the exercise but also to explore our rich and inspiring past. Most certainly you will not be disappointed.

Bob Paterson
North Queensferry
September 2015

WALKING THE WAY

The total distance from Dunsyre to Swanston is around 32 kilometres (20 miles). For some The Way would not be a particularly strenuous day's outing. However, the route is described in three sections to enable those who so choose to take their time to explore their surroundings.

Clearly the route can be followed in either direction, but it is described here from south to north. That progression enables the walker to start on the lower and less demanding sections of the walk and keeps the more dramatic sections and views for later.

Dunsyre Hamlet beneath Dunsyre Hill

It is not possible to reach the starting point at Dunsyre by bus, nor is there suitable parking at Dunsyre. Ideally, the walker should arrange to be dropped off at Dunsyre or, alternatively, start from Dolphinton which is on a bus route. Stagecoach routes 101 and 102 run from Edinburgh to Dumfries and stop at several locations in Edinburgh, Flotterstone, Silverburn, Carlops, West Linton and Dolphinton.

Although the Pentlands are not high hills by Scottish standards several stretches of the route are exposed. Good walking boots and warm, waterproof clothing are essential, along with a rucksack with food, drink, spare clothing, a map and compass. A camera, guidebook, walking pole and mobile phone may be useful accessories, although mobile phone coverage is patchy. While some Pentland days can be idyllic others can be cold, windy and wet in any season. Check the weather before you start, but remember that hill weather can be changeable.

The Way is covered by the Ordnance Survey Landranger maps 66 and 72 or Explorer sheet 344. The maps which accompany this book are illustrative and not suitable for detailed navigation. The whole route lies close to the A702 which is the obvious escape route in case of difficulty.

Following The Way is fairly straightforward. It consists of a variety of long established tracks and paths and signs and waymarkers have been positioned by several organisations including The Scottish Rights of Way and Access Society (ScotWays), Tweed Trails and the Pentland Hills Regional Park. It has also been waymarked by the Friends of the Pentlands as shown below.

Waymarker

In the text route-finding information is shown in blue. The text in italics refers to places close to but not on The Way. This information is included as it may help the walker to explore places of interest close to The Way.

For those who wish to take their time there are catering facilities available at West Linton, Carlops, Flotterstone and Swanston. Bed and breakfast accommodation is available at Ingraston, Dolphinton; West Linton; the Allan Ramsay, Carlops and Patie's Hill and Peggy's Lea at Nine-Mile-Burn. Further details are provided on the map which accompanies this publication.

The Pentlands have a long history of unhindered access to responsible walkers largely because of their proximity to Edinburgh, but also because walkers have, generally, behaved responsibly. The Land Reform (Scotland) Act 2003 provides everyone with the right to be on most land and inland water for recreation providing they act responsibly. Access rights and responsibilities are explained fully in the Scottish Outdoor Access Code (see www.outdooraccess-scotland.com).

- The key things to do are:
- Take responsibility for your own actions
- Respect the interests of others
- Care for your environment
- Use gates and stiles to cross fences
- Leave gates as you found them
- Keep dogs under control

Walkers are also encouraged to embrace the maxim: 'Take nothing but photographs – leave nothing but footprints'.

The Pentlands are a working environment and are used extensively for sheep and cattle husbandry, arable crops and game shooting. Special care needs to be taken during lambing (March to May) and the tupping (breeding) season in November. Dogs should not be taken into fields with lambs or calves and must be kept under close control in fields with other animals. Dogs can also be a hazard to ground-nesting birds in May and June.

Jacob Sheep at Ingraston Farm

Grouse can be shot from 12 August to 10 December, partridge from 1 September to 1 February and pheasant from 1 October to 1 February. As grouse shoots have become fewer because of a lack of birds, especially in the Regional Park, pheasant and particularly partridge shoots have increased on the lower lying farms. Shoots are usually well signed and the line of the drive obvious. Always obey any signs, or instructions, given by persons managing the shoot.

Part of the northern Pentlands is owned by the Ministry of Defence and is used for both live firing and military training exercises. The firing range is on the south side of Castlelaw Hill and is well marked with red flags or lights. Responsible access is not usually affected by training exercises but again walkers must obey temporary signs or instructions for their own safety.

Red Grouse

The Pentlands contain a variety of wildlife although some of it may be difficult to spot. Grasslands are home to brown hares, short-eared owls, common shrew and meadow brown and ringlet butterflies. Heather moorland is home to red grouse, mountain hares, buzzards and merlin.

A variety of wildfowl can be seen on or near the various reservoirs. The North Esk Reservoir has a noisy colony of black-headed gulls. West Water Reservoir is a Site of Special Scientific Interest (SSSI) and a Ramsar site (a wetland of international importance) and is home to thousands of over-wintering pink-footed geese. Mallard, teal, whooper swan and crested grebe can be found at Threipmuir and Bavelaw Marsh. The wooded areas around the periphery of the hills support sparrowhawk, goldcrest, tree creeper, crossbill and willow warbler, while patches of scrub are good places to see robin, wren, stonechat and whinchat.

Peacock butterfly exploring catkins

DUNSYRE TO CARLOPS

The first section of The Way is from Dunsyre to Carlops via West Linton golf course. The distance is approximately 12 kilometres. Following the route, which is largely on wide tracks, is straightforward, although some care needs to be taken around Garvald.

Dunsyre

Before setting out on the Way the walker may wish to explore the nearby attraction of Little Sparta.

The garden of the late Ian Hamilton Finlay at Little Sparta is unique and well worth a visit, not least because it contrasts so starkly with the surrounding countryside. The garden is at the former farm of Stonypath (NT055488) and there is a small car park at NT057483 where an un-surfaced track heads north-west from the road from Dunsyre to Newbigging. It is about half a kilometre from the car park to the garden and sturdy footwear is required.

The Little Sparta website describes the garden as "a place for contemplation, intellectual receptiveness and enjoyment. The garden as a whole discloses to the viewer who walks round it many complexities of meaning, sentiment and wit." The garden is not open in the winter and has limited opening hours in the summer. To find out more visit: www.littlesparta.co.uk

The Pentlands, and perhaps especially the Dunsyre area, have strong connections with the 17th century Covenanting movement. The movement sprang up in protest at Charles I's attempts to dictate the way in which Scots should worship and brought the majority of Scotland's population into direct conflict with the king and his adherence to Divine Right. On 28 February 1638 the National Covenant was adopted and signed by a large gathering in Greyfriars Kirk in Edinburgh. The subscribers engaged, by oath, to maintain religion in the form that it had existed in 1580 – a position which had been endorsed by James VI. The Covenanters raised an army to resist Charles I's religious reforms and defeated him in the Bishops Wars of 1639-40. The crisis that this caused to the Stuart monarchy was a contributing factor in the subsequent outbreak of the English and Scottish civil wars.

When Charles II returned from exile in 1660 he renounced the Covenants, which were declared unlawful oaths, and the king's attempt to restore Episcopacy led to rebellious ministers holding services in the countryside known as 'conventicles'. Attendance at conventicles was made a capital offence and that led to an outbreak of armed rebellion in 1666. Throughout the period of repression the Covenanters continued to hold their convictions and it is estimated that between 1661 and 1680 some 18,000 Covenanters were killed.

Before setting out on The Way the walker should take time to visit Dunsyre's pretty little church with its interesting grave stones. With the closure of the railway in 1945, the track of which is clearly visible, Dunsyre slipped back into its

Dunsyre Church

earlier tranquillity. However, the cultivation terraces on Dunsyre Hill are early evidence of man's association with the area as they date from prehistoric times through to the medieval period. Unusually the settlement is named after the hill rather than the other way round. Gaelic *dun siar* meaning 'western hill-fort'.

Dunsyre church is a perfect location to stop and reflect on the Covenanters, not least because many conventicles were held in the surrounding hills. For centuries Dunsyre was a religious centre and some claim that the present church was built on ground once used for Druid worship. In the late 1100s the church was associated with the monastery at Kelso, founded by Tironesian monks from Chartres, in France, in 1128. By the early 1600s, however, the church was strongly Presbyterian and the grave of minister William Somervell, who died in 1646, can be found in the churchyard.

Just a kilometre to the south-east of Dunsyre is Newholm (NT081476) which was the home of Major Joseph Learmont who was the leader of the Covenanters troop of horse at the battle of Rullion Green in 1666. He survived the battle and was again in the field at the battle of Bothwell Bridge in 1679. However, in 1682 he was arrested and sentenced to imprisonment on the Bass Rock. Luckily, he was released following the Glorious Revolution in 1688.

He died at Newholm in 1693 at the age of eighty eight and his life is commemorated on a plaque in Blackmount Parish Church, formerly known as Dolphinton Church, at NT101464.

Will Grant[3] tells us of the secret passage at Newholm which enabled persecuted preachers to escape to a room sunk underground outside the house. The Reverend Donald Cargill was not one of those lucky preachers. He preached his last sermon at Dunsyre and shortly afterwards was arrested, taken to Edinburgh, and hanged in the Grassmarket in 1681.

Dunsyre Mains

The Way begins in Dunsyre where a ScotWays finger post by Dunsyre Mains (NT073482) indicates that it is just 3 kilometres to Garvald. Two Pentland Way markers can be found close to the finger post. Head along the metalled road, with the cultivation terraces on Dunsyre Hill clearly visible on the left. Where the road to Easton Farm turns left keep straight ahead on a wide unsurfaced track. After nearly a kilometre the track crosses the Medwin Water and climbs up past two metal gates.

---

3 Grant, p44

Dunsyre Hill

COVENANTER'S GRAVE

At the second metal gate at NT094495 there is a ScotWays finger post indicating the path to Crosswood via the Covenanter's Grave. The grave is at NT078523 and can be reached by following a path that runs north-west across the flank of Cairn Knowe and then on to Black Law. The grave lies some 3.5 kilometres from the track between Dunsyre and Garvald. Although the terrain is somewhat featureless there is a line of sight posts to assist navigation.

The small headstone on Black Law marks the spot where a Covenanter, thought to be John Carphin, was buried. He was wounded at Rullion Green in 1666 but escaped and made his way through the hills to the former shepherd's cottage at Blackhill (NT088516), now a ruin, where he rested. The Covenanter requested that, should he die, he be buried within sight of the Ayrshire hills, his home county. The shepherd, Adam Sanderson, carried the body to a spot from where the distant hill of Cairn Table, a little south of Muirkirk, is visible.

Covenanter's Grave

The present stone was erected in 1841 by the Reverend Dr Manuel of Dunsyre. The inscription reads: 'Sacred to the memory of a Covenanter who fought and was wounded at Rullion Green Nov 28th 1666 and who died at Oaken Bush the day after the battle and was buried here by Adam Sanderson of Blackhill." The original stone was inscribed simply 'COVENANTER DUNSYRE 1666', and is now located within Blacklaw Parish Church.

Returning to The Way, a little beyond the second metal gate with the ScotWays sign, the walker will find a Pentland Way marker on a short post on the left. The marker indicates that the walker should leave the broad track and head to the right on a faint track that leads gently down to the Medwin Water. The bridge across the Water at NT096493 soon becomes visible, but take care when approaching it as the ground can be boggy in wet weather.

An earlier footbridge was installed here by The Friends of the Pentlands in late 2005. The work was undertaken by a contractor with funding coming from the Dulverton Trust and South Lanarkshire Council. Unfortunately, it was damaged by flood in 2012 but, thanks to the generosity of the James Thin Trust, a replacement bridge was opened in the spring of 2014.

Garvald Bridge

Once over the footbridge, cross the stile and head along the small field keeping the fence on the right. Take care not to disturb any animals. Go through the metal gate at the end of the field, cross another stile and follow a rough, short path skirting Garvald Home Farm with a fence on its right. Garvald Home Farm is a centre for adults with learning difficulties. They would enjoy a chat if you can spare a few moments.

Garvald Home Farm

At the end of the path go through a wooden gate and, carefully, go down three steep, stone steps. The walker is now alongside a Tweed Trails finger-post. Follow the sign pointing to West Linton.

Follow the broad track which shortly leads between two old, stone gate pillars as you cross the Garvald Burn. Soon you approach two new stone gate pillars where you keep right. Keep the attractive small pond on your right and the building known as Ferniehaugh on your left.

The farm steading of Medwynbank lies just to the west of Ferniehaugh and the traditional fiddle tune 'The High Road to Linton' was composed by Dickson of Medwynbank some time ago. The 'Road' referred to is the Roman Road shown on today's maps, of which more later. Dickson was one of generations of millwrights and joiners associated with Medwynbank, which is still home to a saw-mill. In the past the surrounding clachan supported a mixture of spinners, weavers, dyers and wheelwrights.

Ferniehaugh

Just beyond Ferniehaugh, where the track curves round behind the house, go straight on through the wooden gate. The gate post bears a ScotWays sign for West Linton. Follow the rough track leading out towards the open moor with trees on your right. Once on the moor the track leads steadily north-eastwards, initially running parallel to the Garvald Burn, to North Slipperfield (NT128517).

DOLPHINTON

Dolphinton is an alternative start point for The Way and has the advantage that it can be reached by bus. There is also limited car parking space.

Dolphinton lies partly in the Scottish Borders and partly in South Lanarkshire. The name is part Old Norse, personal name Dolgfinnr, plus Scots – toun, meaning farm. However, it is often claimed that it gets its name from Dolphine, elder brother of the first earl of Dunbar, who was granted the land in the 12th century. The estate was owned by the Brown family from the 16th to the 19th centuries and, thereafter, it passed to the MacKenzie family by marriage.

The MacKenzies built a new manor in the early 1880s, now Dolphinton House (NT101467), purchased the lands of Kippit and made the property at Meadowhead (NT102461) into a summer house. The monument on Kippit Hill (NT111477) is dedicated to the memory of Kenneth MacKenzie of Dolphinton, who was killed near Arras in France on 27 August 1918.

Surprisingly in view of its size, Dolphinton was served by two railways in the 19th century. The Leadburn, Linton and Dolphinton Railway reached the village in 1864 and in 1867 Dolphinton was linked to Carstairs.

Monument on Kippit Hill

This alternative start point for The Way begins at the northern outskirts of Dolphinton at the junction of the A702 and the unclassified road signposted Dunsyre 3 miles and Garvald 1 mile, just below the monument on Kippit Hill at NT111478.

From the start point follow the unclassified road towards Dunsyre. After about half a kilometre you come to Karécole Farm Steadings on your right. Go through the wooden bridle gate to the left of the main gate to the Steading and follow a way-marked trail that leads to the Garvald lodge house at NT103485. Thereafter, follow the metalled road to Garvald for about 1 kilometre, but beware of traffic as the road is narrow.

At Garvald the alternative first section joins the main line of The Way which starts from Dunsyre. At the Tweed Trails finger post at NT098493, by Garvald Home Farm, turn right and follow the track for West Linton.

Once past Ferniehaugh, and just off The Way to the left, there are two cairns, dating from the 2nd millennium BC, both of which are marked on the map (NT105503 and NT110509). According to Baldwin[4] "these are part of a remarkable collection of nine or so round burial cairns, clustered around the 280 m contour. The Nether Cairn, over 15 m in diameter and 3.7 m high, is one of the best preserved, reasonably accessible, round cairns in the area. About 1 m beyond the present base are slight indications of a surrounding ditch about 1.8 m wide. The Upper Cairn, by contrast, some 730 m north-east, is even larger – over 20 m across and 4.2 m high.

"This chain of large, round, prehistoric burial cairns in the Dolphinton-West Linton area seems to mark an important prehistoric route linking the upper Clyde valley with the Forth estuary."

---

4   Baldwin, p202.

During 2006 the Friends of the Pentlands undertook a major way-marking project in the south-west Pentlands with guidance from the Scottish Rights of Way and Access Society (ScotWays) and the co-operation of local landowners and land managers. The 'schedule of tasks' listed 78 specific items and included the renewal of seven signposts, 26 line of sight posts, 15 way-marking posts and five new gates.

Hard at Work

That work greatly improved access to the old cross-Pentland rights of way from Tarbrax (NT0255) and Boston Cottage (NT021516), close to the A70, to West Linton. Scottish Natural Heritage provided a grant of £3,000 to purchase materials and the Friends made available a further £1,000 from its own funds. The work was carried out by volunteers and amounted to some 550 hours.

Just beyond the Upper Cairn the route passes Rumbling Well, the source of the Garvald Burn. This unremarkable spot marks the watershed, which is part of Scotland's national watershed. The Garvald Burn runs south-west and, eventually, runs into the Clyde. About 500 metres ahead the path picks up the Lowsmeadow Burn which, eventually, runs into the Tweed and ultimately into the North Sea.

There has recently been some development at North Slipperfield, including the creation of a small loch for fishing. It is a mixed sports estate which offers shooting of grouse, pheasant, partridge, duck and geese. It also offers rough shooting of rabbit, snipe and woodcock.

Just to the north of the track lies West Water Reservoir, completed in 1967. The site is of international importance as a winter roost for pink-footed geese and is also home to common gulls and breeding waders, including dunlin and ringed plover. In July 1992 a combination of wave erosion and low water level led to the discovery of an early Bronze Age cemetery at West Water. The remains of seven cists in varying conditions were recovered. In addition to human remains, food vessels, flint tools and beads of coal, lead and bone were found. It is thought that the find of lead beads might be the earliest evidence of the use of metallic lead in Britain.

Just to the north of the buildings at North Slipperfield are the remains of a Roman marching camp. The Roman Road, which The Way joins at NT138517, ran from the western end of Hadrian's Wall, near Carlisle, to the fortified Roman port at Cramond on the Forth. At the point where The Way joins the Roman Road there is an interesting information panel at the right of the path.

Mendick Hill from the Roman Road

A little further on, and off to the left, there is a grassy mound which contains the seven re-sited Bronze Age burial cists from West Water Reservoir. There is a good interpretation panel at the site so it is worth taking time to locate it. It lies between the track and the golf course. Some 4,000 years ago bodies were not 'laid out' for burial but were buried as they died in a curled up-position. Three of the cists contained fossil pollen, grains of meadowsweet (*filipendula ulmaria*), also known as Queen of the Meadow. Meadowsweet has very occasionally been found in other Bronze Age burials. In the 16th century it was customary to cover floors with rushes and herbs to give warmth and overcome smells and meadowsweet was the favourite choice of Elizabeth I for that purpose.

Bronze Age Burial Cist

In 2013 the Friends of the Pentlands planted a small arboretum alongside the burial cists consisting of 21 different native trees including beech, hawthorn, juniper, rowan and silver birch. This arboretum is one of five planted by the Friends at sites in the Pentlands.

From North Slipperfield The Way follows the unclassified road that runs through West Linton golf course until, adjacent to the Golf Club, it reaches the unclassified road that runs from West Linton to Baddinsgill. Turn left onto this road and then right after 200 metres onto the road that is sign-posted Carlops 2½ miles.

The road that runs from West Linton to the Cauldstane Slap via Baddinsgill roughly follows the line of a formerly important drove road. Drove roads were not roads as we know them today but rather routes between key points where the drovers, or their cattle, chose their own route. Drovers brought sheep and cattle from the major trysts at Falkirk and Crieff to sell at the Linton markets and purchased the once famous Linton breed of sheep, which were then driven north to the Ochil Hills and Highlands. Linton sheep, which were black-faced and black-legged with short bodies and coarse wool, were very popular for their hardiness and sweet meat.

Droving was at its height in the early 19th century when upwards of 30,000 sheep would be sold annually at the Linton markets. Many of the sheep would be driven south for sale in markets in the north of England. The once popular expression 'big as a Linton market' indicates the former importance of this activity.

At one time there was a move to make the route over the Cauldstane Slap into a turnpike road. The inhabitants on the north side of the pass were happy with that proposal. The Earl of Morton, however, objected to a highway traversing his lands and the project was dropped.

The 'Slap' is also known as 'The Thieves' Road', not an uncommon name for a drove road, there was money to be made by stealing cattle. Border Reivers, Moss Troopers (disbanded soldiers or deserters who kept their weapons and lived a life of banditry) and other robbers galloped through the pass on night raids. To combat the threat the drovers slept beside their cattle and were quick to resist with staff and dirk. Nevertheless cattle were stolen and blood was spilt. Cairns Castle, the ruins of which can still be seen at the western end of Harperrig Reservoir, was the

Cairns Castle Ruins

stronghold of the self-styled Warden of the Slap who, with little success, endeavoured to make money by protecting those using the pass. The castle was built in the 15th century for the Crichton family of Cairns and is now the home of numerous jackdaws.

It is thought that James IV travelled over the Slap in November 1490 after buying a horse in Linlithgow. Today the route is a Heritage Path.

WEST LINTON

Although West Linton is not on The Way the walker may well choose to visit it in search of food and drink or to explore its attractions. It may be small but it is old and full of interest. (See www.westlinton.org.uk)

From the golf course West Linton is just a kilometre away and it can be reached by walking down Medwyn Road but, if you have a head for heights, far better to approach it via the Cat Walk – see page 37.

The settlement is named 'Lyintoun' on Blaeu's map of 1654 - literally the farm beside the Lyne Water. The village of Linton is of ancient origin. The first written record of the settlement dates from the 12th century when the church of 'Linton-Ridric' was gifted to the Church of St Mary of Kelso. The reference to 'Ridric' is to Rhydderch Hael (Roderick the Liberal), King of Strathclyde, contemporary and friend of St Columba and supporter of Kentigern, more commonly known as St Mungo, the first Bishop of Glasgow. Roderick defeated the pagans in Liddesdale in 573 and subsequently established Christianity in the area. Roderick died in 603 and for many years the village was known as Linton Roderick. The addition of 'West' was adopted much later to distinguish the settlement from East Linton in East Lothian.

The church stands on the site of the former church and its manse. The current graveyard contains many interesting grave stones including the burial sites of the Lawsons of Cairnmuir and the Douglases of Garvaldfoot.

On the lower green, adjacent to the church, stands an excellent information panel and alongside it stands the old toll house, now a café. The toll house was built in the early nineteenth century and tolls were levied on travellers, including the drovers and their animals, passing through the district. The ticket issued entitled the traveller to free passage through other districts, provided he did so on the same day. Anyone attempting to bypass the toll could be fined twenty shillings (£1.00) and there were severe penalties for damaging a toll house. Toll charges ceased in 1863.

The Old Manor House, at the top of the High Street, dates from 1578. In the 1600s James Gifford was one of Linton's bailies. He was a farmer and self-styled sculptor of some considerable ability. About 1660 he created the 'Gifford Stone' which is now displayed on the gable end of a house opposite the Raemartin Hotel in the High Street.

The stone bears a modern plaque stating 'Carved c1660 by James Gifford, Stonemason, Sculptor and Proportioner of West Linton'.

West Linton Church

The Gifford Stone

He also erected a cross in memory of his wife and five children. Will Grant tells us that Gifford created a cross with symbols representing his wife and four children believing his family to be complete. His delight about becoming a father again was tempered by his need to include an effigy of the new-born child and he did so by placing it on the mother's head.[5] Subsequently the figures fell and disappeared. However, the figure of Gifford's beloved wife survived and a replica of that statue has now been set in the face of the clock tower, formerly the village well. The original is now housed in a glass fronted alcove within the nearby village hall, The Grahan Institute. Linton was raised to a Burgh of Regality in 1631 giving it the right to hold fairs and markets. By the end of the 18th century there were between twenty and thirty looms in the village. That figure rose to about eighty in the early 19th century, some weaving household goods, but most weaving cotton cloth for Edinburgh and Glasgow merchants. In 1834 there were five tailors in the village, four dressmakers, two butchers, five carriers, nine retailers of meal, groceries and spirits, two surgeons and four innkeepers.

---

5   See Grant p64

In 1864 West Linton was connected to the Leadburn to Dolphinton railway which was linked to the Edinburgh to Peebles line. It was built to support mining and quarrying activities in the area but it also led to wealthy Edinburgh people building houses in the village, either as a summer home or as a residence, within commuting distance of Edinburgh. The last passenger service was in 1933. The second half of the 20th century saw a surge in new housing which led to the doubling of the population.

West Linton Clock Tower

The walker returning to The Way from West Linton should do so via The Loan. This path, which is signed, starts opposite the Gordon Arms on the A702 at NT149520 and joins The Way at NT142526.

Returning to The Way we pick it up again at NT140523, at the junction of the road signed Carlops 2½ miles and the unclassified road from West Linton to Baddinsgill. The next section of The Way, which leads to Carlops, runs parallel to the Roman Road. Following the route is straightforward; however, there is much to hold the interest of the walker.

THE ROMAN ROAD

The Roman Road, with its attendant marching camps, was built by the Legions under Agricola about 80AD. However, as it follows the natural route lying to the east of the Pentlands, it remained a highway until superseded by the A702 in 1833. Perhaps unsurprisingly there are many tales of diverse travellers.

In the 12th century the lands of Slipperfield were granted to the Augustinian monks of Holyrood. The boundary of those lands was the West Water, then known as the Pollentarf, and to mark that delineation a cross once stood at the point where the Roman Road crosses the West Water. The bridge that stands at this point today dates from 1620, although it was restored in 1899[6].

It is recorded that in 1334 William Douglas, Knight of Liddesdale, ravaged the lands of Lothian while operating from lairs in the Pentland Hills. In 1398 his kinsman, George Douglas, Earl of Angus, mounted a campaign against James Douglas of Dalkeith, one of whose estates was West Linton. While the Black Douglasses were better known for border feuding it is clear that their warlike activities extended into the area of the Pentlands and, without doubt, their marauding bands would have travelled up and down the Roman Road.

Bridge over West Water

There are also records of Mary, Queen of Scots, with her husband Lord Darnley leading an army along this route from Edinburgh to

The bridge is at NT135514, a short distance from The Way.

Biggar in October 1565. Grant[7] tells us that: "She rode a stately charger, and had a pair of pistols stuck in the holsters at her saddle bows; and it is said her scarlet and embroidered riding-dress covered a suit of defensive armour, and that under her hood and veil she wore a steel casque, while Darnley wore a suit of gilt armour."

The Roman Road was also travelled by pilgrims en route to the shrine of St Ninian at Whithorn in Wigtonshire. The most important of those was James IV and the history of the Priory provides details of the king's pilgrimages. In 1507 James was deeply troubled by the fact that his queen, Margaret, daughter of Henry VI of England, and infant son, the future James V, had both fallen ill and he attributed their misfortune to his sins. With a small party he set out on foot and reached Whithorn in just eight days. When the queen and the young prince recovered James believed this to be due to the blessing of St Ninian. James's pilgrimages are well documented and form the most complete records of individual pilgrimage in medieval Scotland and confirm that he travelled on the Roman Road on his journey to Whithorn.

Medwyn House (NT142523) lies close to the starting point of this section of The Way. This is the site of the former Brig House Inn which became the location of the Linton fairs when they became too large to hold on the village green. The Brig House Inn, standing as it did at the junction of the Roman Road and the Drove Road over the Cauldstane Slap, has a long history

It is known that James IV visited Linton in October 1490 and was supplied with funds by the Lord High Treasurer which, quite probably, were spent on music makers at the Inn. James had a passion for music and liked distributing sums to fiddlers, lute players, pipers and story tellers.

---

7   Grant p57

At one time the Inn was owned by James Wedderspuine who was one of those charged with complicity in the murder of David Rizzio, secretary to Mary, Queen of Scots.

Charles X, the last Bourbon King of France, escaped to Britain at the time of the French Revolution in 1792 and, for some time thereafter, lived in Edinburgh and London. During one of his spells in Edinburgh he lodged at the Brig House Inn while hunting on the Slipperfield Moors.

Burns visited the Inn and finding the proprietor away from home inscribed on a window: 'Honest Graeme, aye the same, never to be found at hame!'

With the building of the A702 in the 1830s the Brig House Inn lost its purpose as a coaching inn and subsequently became a private dwelling.

Lynedale House

From the start point the narrow metalled road leads down to the stone bridge which crosses the Lyne alongside Lynedale House. It then ascends steeply until alongside the house called

Tocherknowe where it levels out and enters a more open landscape.

To reach West Linton via the Catwalk look for a small gap in the rhododendrons on your right opposite the paddock alongside Tocherknowe. Climb the steep bank briefly and go through a wooden kissing gate on your right.

The path is narrow and runs high above the Lyne Water through mature woodland giving dramatic glimpses of the Lyne Water through the trees. Take great care, however, a slip here could have serious consequences. The north section of the wood forms part of the grounds of Lynedale House while the larger, southern section is owned by the Woodland Trust Scotland: for more information visit: www.woodlandtrust.org.uk

On the approach to West Linton the path descends by steps and joins the A702 where the Lyne Water flows under the road and next to the bus stop for Edinburgh.

Returning to The Way, just before a path leads off left to Stonypath Farm is the feature known as the Siller Holes (NT144535). There is not much to see here but the inundations and humps on the flank of Lead Law and a small pond in boggy ground. It was the excavation of the pond in 1993, combined with some opportunistic field walking that resulted in the finds of medieval pottery and fragments of garments and shoes. It has been established that silver and lead were mined here in medieval times. Furthermore it has been claimed that Mary of Guise, regent of Scotland from 1554 to 1560, and mother of Mary, Queen of Scots, paid her army with silver from the Siller Holes. The materials collected were subsequently deposited in the National Museum of Scotland. The path now continues up a steepish section. At the top take time to admire the backward view towards Mendick

Hill, which looks deceptively high from this point, and the forward view to the higher tops of Scald Law and the Pentland ridge before descending towards Carlops.

The next building on The Way is Fairslacks, formerly a blacksmith's shop and now a farm. Will Grant recalls how it got its name. When the driver of the stage got down from his seat he enquired of the smith how business was and he invariably got the same reply – "Things are fair slack, fair slack". The nickname was originally given to the smith but is now the name of the property.

Grant also tells of the neighbouring cottages named Waterloo and Trafalgar. The croft of Waterloo was owned by James Knox, a Waterloo veteran and an adjoining crofter took part in the Battle of Trafalgar. Grant states that no trace of these cottages remain; however, their names live on today.

Trafalgar Villa and Waterloo Cottage

A little beyond Fairslacks lies the substantial stone house of Linton Muir on the right and the two cottages on the left are named Trafalgar Villa and Waterloo Cottage. Go straight on through a gate and on the left lies a large modern bungalow called Schiehallion.

A little further on is Windy Gowl Farm which has both Icelandic horses and a herd of Red Aberdeen Angus cattle. To find out more visit: www.phicelandics.co.uk

Icelandic Horses

Just beyond the farm on the left there is a wooden summer house called 'Freedom'. It is worth stopping here to look into the depression on your left which is a section of one of the finest sub-glacial meltwater channels in Scotland. You are looking down on the feature named on the map as Hell's Hole and the raised feature in the middle of the channel is Dun Kaim.

The Way now descends to reach the A702 on the outskirts of Carlops. Take care when crossing the road to reach the pavement as the traffic flow is considerable.

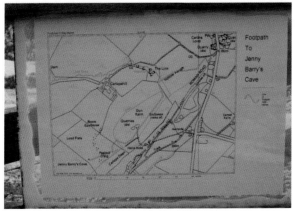

Footpath to Jenny Barry's Cove

If you want a good view of the meltwater channel take the track to the left opposite the car park signed for Carlopshill Farm. About 100 metres along the track there is a metal kissing gate on the left from where there is an excellent view down the length of the channel. The kissing gate also gives access to a path to Jenny Barry's Cove via Dun Kaim and Peaked Craig.

Jenny Barry was one of the infamous Carlops witches, about more of whom later, but the cove is a low rock-hewn tunnel, almost certainly attributable to the work of lead prospectors. To discover more about this feature visit the Quaternary of Scotland at: www.jncc.gov. uk and search for 'Carlops'.

Meltwater Channel

Note the interesting names of the cottages as you walk through Carlops including, on the right – Ashley, The Biggin and Weavers and, on the left - Houlet, Amulree, Ferndale, Finlaggan and Blinieknowe.

This section of The Way ends at the Allan Ramsay Hotel which, conveniently, is close to the bus stop. Should the walker feel the need of food and drink, or just a short rest, the Allan Ramsay may prove to be 'just what the doctor ordered'! To discover more visit: www.allanramsayhotel.com

The Allan Ramsay Hotel

Carlops

The Dulverton Bird Hide, North Esk Reservoir

CARLOPS TO FLOTTERSTONE

Carlops, situated near the source of the North Esk River, grew at the end of the 18th century around the cotton weaving industry. The hand looms ceased to function in the late 19th century and the village became a health resort for summer visitors from Edinburgh. Carlops is closely associated with the house and grounds of Newhall which was purchased by the Edinburgh advocate, Robert Brown, in 1783. It was Brown who established the cotton-weaving industry in Carlops by laying out linear rows of cottages on each side of the main Edinburgh to Biggar road.

However, our interest in the village centres on its witches, an extraordinary shepherdess and the poet who gives his name to the village inn.

Weavers Cottage

The name 'Carlops' is, perhaps, derived from the story of the two local witches, or carlins in old Scots, called Jenny Barry and Mause, who used to jump between two outcrops of rock in the village. Thus the 'carlins' loup' became Carlops.

Carlins' Loup

Jenny Barry we have already met, while Mause was a witch in Allan Ramsay's pastoral drama, *The Gentle Shepherd,* of which more later.

The village's extraordinary shepherdess was Jenny Armstrong who was born at Fairliehope (NT156566) in 1903. Jenny would not have wished to be described as a gentle shepherdess. She was a tough, feisty, independent lady who worked with her dogs in all weathers throughout many a year.

Land above Fairliehope

Jenny would not have been unique, although shephcrdesses were fairly unusual, but it was the distinguished artist, Victoria Crowe, who made Jenny almost immortal. Victoria, a young mother, moved to the hamlet of Kitleyknowe, on the edge of Carlops, from Surrey with her husband in 1970 and Jenny became her neighbour. Despite their age difference the two ladies became friends and soon Victoria was accompanying Jenny on her morning walks, drawing as she went. While Jenny enjoyed Victoria's company she was not initially enthusiastic about being drawn. Victoria's early drawings were of rugged, rural, winter landscapes with stark, leafless, tall trees, dogs and sheep, with Jenny initially featured as a small figure in the background.

Jenny's former Cottage

With the passage of time Jenny became less active and the drawings began to concentrate on Jenny and her simple, small cottage which was belatedly equipped with electricity and a telephone. The final images are of Jenny's ornaments, poignantly painted after her death in 1985.

Probably unwittingly, Victoria Crowe created an intriguing and sensitive visual diary of a now lost way of life. Happily that situation has been preserved for posterity. In 2000 the Scottish National Portrait Gallery decided to celebrate the heroism of everyday life in Scotland in a series of exhibitions and publications, of which *A Shepherd's Life* was the first. The exhibition consisted of 40 paintings of Jenny in the Pentlands and the book which accompanied the exhibition was reprinted for the fourth time in 2013. The latter brings Jenny's remarkable life alive in both words and pictures.

The poet, Allan Ramsay, was born in Leadhills, in what is now South Lanarkshire, in 1686, although he spent most of his life in Edinburgh. He was a bold pioneer in the development of the Scottish literary tradition and wrote in both English and Scots. He created Britain's first lending library and tried, unsuccessfully in the face of considerable opposition from the Calvinist Kirk, to promote theatre in Edinburgh.

One of Ramsay's great work's published in 1725, *The Gentle Shepherd,* is believed to have been set in the Carlops area. The pastoral drama enjoyed very considerable success both in Ramsay's lifetime and for several years after his death. The play contains skilful sections of lyric and song, develops the pastoral genre and fixes it within a Scottish context. It is generally accepted that the work helps make possible Fergusson's (1750-74) Scots pastorals and much of Burns (1759-96) work.

Ramsay was buried in Greyfriars Kirk in Edinburgh in 1758 and his eldest son, also Allan Ramsay, was the famous portrait painter.

The next section of the Way begins at the Allan Ramsay hotel. The pedimented doorpiece and stone forestair characterise the external appearance of the building which may have originated as a wool store and base for the hand loom weaving industry

This section of the Way takes the walker along the main Pentland ridge

The Allan Ramsay Inn Doorpiece

which, although not high by Scottish standards, is exposed to the elements. It offers impressive views, especially to the east.

From the Allan Ramsay hotel the Way initially follows the A702 towards Edinburgh.

View from the old Carlops Bridge

On the edge of the village it is worth taking a very short detour to view Carlops bridge. Turn left to follow a lane signposted 'Buteland by the Bore Stane' and walk down to the old bridge that crosses the North Esk. The property by the bridge is a former water mill and the bridge offers great views of the tumbling North Esk. Look out for dippers and grey wagtails before returning to the busy A702.

Again, take great care as the traffic is heavy and to stay on a pavement it is necessary to cross the road. Just after the sign indicating that the walker has entered Midlothian there is a ScotWays finger-post sign to the left to Nine Mile Burn and a waymarker.

Wanton Wa's Cottage

Go up the steps and onto a narrow path. After about 300 metres the path joins an unclassified road that leads to Nine Mile Burn, about 2 kilometres away. This road follows the route of the old Roman Road. Follow the road past Wanton Wa's cottage where the walker keeps to the left.

This part of The Way crosses land belonging to the Newhall Estate. There has been a house at Newhall (NT175566) since the 13th century. Originally the land was on the edge of a royal forest but gradually the trees and game gave way to sheep farming. Tradition links the site with a monastic house and that may account for the nearby names of Spittal Farm, Monks' Rig and the Font Stone and St Robert's Croft. Spittal is a fairly common place name in Scotland and is associated with a place of refuge for travellers, often provided as part of a religious house.

Newhall belonged to the Crichton family until the 17th century. Thereafter, the estate became the country home of a succession of

Edinburgh doctors and lawyers. In the early 1700s the then owners, Sir David Forbes and his son John, both Edinburgh advocates, built a new house which forms the basis of the current structure.

As we have already learned Robert Brown became the owner in 1783 and, in addition to building Carlops, he instigated significant agricultural improvements including the first potato field in Scotland.

Newhall c1900
©Midlothian Council Local and Family History Library

Brown also put Newhall on the literary map with his 1808 edition of *The Gentle Shepherd*. He extended the house, adding the walled garden and momentos of *The Gentle Shepherd* to the house and grounds. Robert Brown's son, Hugh, commissioned David Bryce, Scotland's pre-eminent Victorian architect, to extend the house in 1850.

John and Tricia Kennedy have owned Newhall since 1998. The estate offers shooting, holiday cottages, fly fishing on the North Esk reservoir, either clay pigeon shooting or a partridge and pheasant shoot and private garden visits. The garden is also open to the public annually as part the Scotland's Gardens programme. To learn more visit: www.newhallestate.co.uk

The walk towards Nine Mile Burn provides great views of Monks' Rig and the hills to the north. Beyond the road to Spittal Farm, and on the left, the walker passes a modern house called St Robert's Croft. St Robert was a Benedictine monk who founded a congregation of Cistercians in 1098.

Monks' Rig

The hamlet of Nine Mile Burn is so named because it is 9 Scots miles (11¾ English miles) from Edinburgh. The building on the corner, on the right, with the date 1811, is the former Habbie's Howe Inn. A ScotWays publication of 1904 (see bibliography) informs us that: "This old established and comfortable Inn has recently been remodelled and refurbished throughout. Tourists, visitors and picnic parties for Habbie's Howe will find this a delightful resting-place, with every comfort combined with moderate charges." We also learn that there was good stabling and ample carriage accommodation and that plain teas cost 9d or 1s, while high teas were available at 1s 6d or 2s.

At the point where the unclassified road turns right there is a

ScotWays signpost by the small car park to 'Balerno by Monks Rig'. Go through the wooden kissing gate adjacent to the field gate and head for another field gate straight ahead. You may have to pick your way carefully as the ground tends to be boggy. At the field gate turn left and head uphill on the path by the dyke for about 300 metres where you will find a stile. Cross the stile and head right along the drystane dyke to a signpost to 'Monks Rig', about 500 metres away. Continue northwards on the path until you reach the Font Stone at NT175592.

The origins of the Font Stone are unclear as Will Grant explains. "Whether it was a Font Stone, a wayside shrine, or a landmark commanding all the country to the south for the pious friar as he journeyed over the hills to Convent or Spittal, who can tell? But there it remains today, and as we stand and

meditate upon it we link ourselves with a visible symbol of the time when the white-robed monk was a familiar figure on the Pentland Hills."[8]

The Font Stone

Continue northwards over the flat top of Cap Law which offers splendid views of West Kip and the Scald Law group. Descend northwards to the base of West Kip where the path crosses the track from Eastside to Balerno.

8   Quoted in Falconer p108

The Path down to The Howe and Loganlee

There is an alternative route on offer at this point. If the walker does not wish to commit to the main ridge there is a rather faint grassy path to the left which leads down to The Howe. From there the walker can continue on the sheltered, metalled road that runs alongside Loganlee and Glencorse reservoirs before meeting up again with the primary route. At NT219639 turn left onto the path that leads up the side of a small copse of trees and after 200 metres turn left again to regain The Way.

West Kip

As the walker begins to ascend West Kip he or she moves onto land belonging to Alastair and Susan Cowan who live at Eastside Farm (NT184603). Alastair, who is a founder member of the Friends of the Pentlands, is the fifth generation of Cowans to rear Blackface sheep on his 1,230 hectare[9] farm which includes the Kips and Scald Law as well as South Black Hill and Hare Hill. The ground is also home to badgers, foxes, peregrine falcons and red grouse.

This hill farm is ideal for the hardy Blackface ewes that live with their young, immature hoggs (one year old sheep), on the unfenced hill in groups of a few hundred known as hefts. Each heft recognises its own territory which it regards as 'home' and knows where to find

9   1,230 hectares is the equivalent of 2,000 football pitches

the best food and shelter. As this is relatively poor upland pasture each ewe needs about a hectare (1½ football pitches) to survive.

The tupping (mating) season begins in November. Before the season begins the tups (males) are brought into the shed at the farm steading so that the start of the breeding season is controlled. In mid-November the tups are introduced to the ewes. Each tup will service about 60-70 ewes over a period of about six weeks and, as the ewes' gestation period is five months, the lambs are born from mid-April onwards when, hopefully, the weather is getting warmer and the grazing is getting richer.

Badgers

Eastside Farm

The whole herd gets a health check during the winter with each heft being brought down to the handling pens by the shepherd with the help of his dogs and quad bike. The barren ewes and their hoggs are returned to the hill to allow the shepherd to concentrate on the pregnant ewes which are put into the fields on the lower ground to lamb. Some of the hefts e.g. those on Hare Hill, are left to lamb on the hill as they have no cultivated fields within their heft or territory to lamb in. This is no hardship for the ewe (being a wild hill sheep she probably prefers it) but it creates more work for the shepherd.

Lambing starts in mid-April and finishes towards the end of May. The great majority of ewes have a single lamb and give birth without need of intervention. However, it is very important that the ewes are not disturbed by dogs or hill walkers at this stage as that can disturb the bonding process and cause the ewe to reject her lamb. Nevertheless, some lambs are stillborn and some die. On the other hand some ewes will give birth to two lambs but sometimes they do not have sufficient milk to ensure that both survive. That situation can be overcome by 'twinning on' which can be a lifesaver for a hungry lamb. The dead lamb is skinned and its skin placed over a lamb whose mother is unable to provide sufficient milk for it. The ewe whose own lamb has died will accept the 'twinned on' lamb as its own because it smells correct and so there is a satisfactory outcome for both mother and baby.

Blackface Ewe

By June the new lambs will have quadrupled their body weight and they are robust enough to be tagged with the farm's unique code. Clipping, or shearing, begins in June and starts with the previous year's hoggs, followed by the ewes in mid-July. The sheep are ready to be clipped by this stage as they have grown new wool called a 'rise' which is easier for the shearer to clip through. As long as the sheep are held in a position sitting on their haunches they will remain still while being clipped. Blackface sheep have thick coats and produce an abundance of wool, but it is coarse and is usually used to make carpets. The fleece is also rich in lanolin which is extracted and used in the production of face and hand cream.

By the time the annual sheep sales start in early autumn the farm will be home to some 3,000 sheep, and it is necessary to reduce that number considerably before the winter sets in. This ensures there is enough grazing for the remaining stock to remain fit and healthy. The ewes are sold after five years on the farm to low-ground farmers for cross breeding and about half of the ewe lambs are also sold, with the best 400 ewe lambs being retained to replace the older ewes leaving the farm. Some male lambs are kept for breeding while others are sold to low-ground farmers for fattening and meat production.

To discover more about Eastside Farm and its associated holiday cottages visit: www.eastsidecottages.co.uk

Scald Law

View from Scald Law

The Way continues by tackling the steep, but thankfully short, ascent of West Kip the most exposed and shapely of the Pentland peaks. Route finding for the walker continuing on the principal route is straight forward, if rather strenuous. For the next 5 kilometres just stay on the well-defined path which follows the ridge line. After ascending West Kip move on to East Kip and then make the descent and subsequent ascent to the summit of Scald Law the highest point on the Way at 579 metres.

In benign conditions the summit of Scald Law is a place for rest and reflection. The view across the tranquil and prosperous Lothians and Borders countryside belies an often troubled and violent past. The coastal route from Berwick to Edinburgh was the historic invasion route and in the past it was well trodden. Indeed, following the defeat of the Scots by an English army at Neville's Cross in 1346, after which king David II was captured, Carlops was, albeit briefly, on the Scotland England border.

While still on the summit of Scald Law the walker might like to turn to the west and contemplate on something much closer in both distance and time – The Howe at NT190620.

In 2012 John Stirling, then Chairman of the Friends of the Pentlands, and the author visited fellow member Bill Rae at his request to let him record his memories of The Howe. Although Bill lived in Edinburgh he was a frequent visitor to The Howe in the 1930s.

The Howe Today

In those days The Howe consisted of a kitchen, living room and a small bedroom while half the un-wallpapered attic housed a double and single bed and the other half provided storage for animal feed. There was an outside dry toilet and today's garage was then a byre that housed a cow, the shepherd's dogs and, in the loft, some two dozen chickens. The water supply was from a spring which fed a tank in the kitchen where there was a wood burning stove.

Weather permitting there were weekly visits by van from the butcher, grocer and baker, but the kitchen contained a large meal chest which provided emergency rations when snow closed the road. Bill remembered that the cow was a source of butter as well as milk; that there were four large butcher's hooks in the kitchen ceiling for hanging meat; that each year two piglets were purchased, one for fattening and selling on and the other for fattening and then slaughter. The garden provided potatoes, turnips and cabbage.

Bill learnt to fly fish, to watch the swallows to see if the fish were rising, and to snare rabbits. He remembered the joys of mutton broth and curds and whey and beating at grouse shoots for 4s 6d per day, plus tea and cake. In his day a bag of 100 brace was not uncommon. Things have changed and grouse are far less plentiful than they were.

From Scald Law The Way heads north-east zigzagging steeply downhill on a stony path to the bealach where it crosses the Kirk Road path from Penicuik to Balerno.

From Scald Law looking towards Carnethy Hill

Falconer tells us this about the Kirk Road: "The people of Logan Valley would walk over this Old Kirk Road pass to church in Penicuik every Sabbath and coffins would be borne over the same route – quite a last journey. Ten kilometres, with an ascent and descent of 670m, it is a good walk every week. The parish of Penicuik swelled in numbers when the populations of Bavelaw and Logan valley were added. When a census was conducted, the surveyor was granted the use of a pony to enable him to travel through the parish."[10]

Having crossed the Kirk Road, now a Heritage Trail, ascend steeply to the summit of Carnethy Hill with its large cairn.

The Kirk Road

From the summit of Carnethy descend again to a shallow dip before climbing to the cairn on Turnhouse Hill. From the summit follow the well-trodden path, steep in parts, down towards the wooden bridge over Glencorse Burn at NT228631.

10   Falconer pp68-69

Turnhouse Hill from Glencorse Burn

Below the summit of Turnhouse Hill, at NT215626, lies the site of the battle of Rullion Green. The battle, on 28 November 1666, marked the sad and bloody end of the brief Pentland Rising which had its origins in the south-west. Initially the Covenanters numbered some 3,000 and they decided to head to Edinburgh to make representation against their harsh treatment. The force, however, was clearly seen as a threat by the government. By the time the force got to Colinton, on the outskirts of Edinburgh, its numbers had halved, partly due to abysmal weather and partly because it became increasingly clear that their cause had little, if any, support. Finding Edinburgh's gates closed they decided to return home not knowing that General Thomas Dalziel of the Binns had been instructed to march against them.

On the fateful day the Covenanter's commander, Colonel Wallace, decided to review his remaining troops at Rullion Green in an effort to improve their morale and reduce the desertion rate. When horsemen were seen coming from the west their spirits rose at the prospect of reinforcements.

Such euphoria was short lived – it was Dalziel with a force of 3,000 who quickly scattered the remaining 900 Covenanters.

Some 50 Covenanters were killed during the battle, perhaps as many as 100 were taken prisoner and it is thought that others, after fleeing the battle, died from their wounds. Some of the prisoners were treated harshly, despite having been given quarter on the battlefield. About 30 were hanged at the Mercat Cross in Edinburgh and others at various places in the south-west as a warning to others.

Memorial at Rullion Green

It is interesting to note that in 1866, when Robert Louis Stevenson was just 16 his first publication was *The Pentland Rising; A Page of History, 1666.*

House O' Muir, on the A 702 just below Rullion Green, was for long the site of a major annual sheep market. Grant tells us that in 1661 Charles II conferred to the town of Edinburgh the privilege of a market at "the House of the Moore in the paroch of Glencorce". The last market was held in 1871.

Once over the Glencorse Burn The Way continues by turning left and heading towards the old filter beds. However, should the walker wish to stop at Flotterstone then turn right once across the Glencorse Burn and head through a gate to the metalled road. On the road turn right again and after about half a kilometre the Flotterstone Inn is on the right. The Inn provides sustenance and shelter and is close to the bus stop for Edinburgh.
Visit: www.flotterstoneinn.com

Flotterstone Inn

Tree at Kirkton Cottage

FLOTTERSTONE TO SWANSTON

The third and final section of The Way takes the walker from Flotterstone to Swanston. This is the shortest section of The Way, less than 5 kilometres, but it is the most varied part of the route. Its highlight is the great view from the summit of Allermuir over Scotland's capital and the spectacular panorama to the north. It ends at the picturesque hamlet of Swanston and its association with Robert Louis Stevenson.

Castlelaw Fort

Before tackling this part of The Way the walker might like to explore the hill fort at Castlelaw and the Tytler Memorial above Woodhouselee. Both these sites are close to the small car park at NT231637.

Castlelaw fort and souterrain (NT229638) dates from the 1st-2nd century AD. Baldwin[11] tells us that: "The oval fort was originally

---

11   Baldwin p172

surrounded by a palisaded enclosure, later succeeded by a simple rampart mainly of plain clay but reinforced with timber by the entrance.

Late in its occupation, just before the Romans arrived in AD 79 or 80, further defences were added, and it was in the ditch between the two later ramparts, at the north-east end of the fort, that a well-preserved souterrain was subsequently built."

The fort pre-dates the Roman occupation, although the discovery of Roman pottery indicates that the Romans made use of it. However, it seems to have been subsequently re-occupied by the Britons.

The Tytler memorial lies about half a kilometre north-east of the Castlelaw car park at NT234644. The Fraser Tytlers, a prominent family of Edinburgh lawyers who were also distinguished historians and writers and patrons of the arts, were the lairds of Woodhouselee from 1748 to 1922. Alexander Fraser Tytler was raised to the bench in 1801 and took his seat as Lord Woodhouselee. He was also a patron of Burns. At his request Burns removed the following lines from an early draft of 'Tam O'Shanter'.

"Three lawyers' tongues, turn'd inside out,
Wi lies seam'd like a beggars clout;
Three priests' hearts, rotten black as muck
Lay stinking, vile in every neuk."

Woodhouselee had its ghost. Lady Anne Bothwellhaugh lived at old Woodhouselee which was burned to the ground on the orders of James VI's Regent, Moray. Lady Anne was turned out into the woods with her child where she went mad and perished. The stories of her haunting both old and new Woodhouselee survived over two and a half centuries and were well known to Sir Walter Scott who was a frequent visitor to the property.

The Ornamental Plinth

The memorial, which is some 18 feet tall, was erected in 1893 to the memory of James Stuart Tytler, the 4ᵗʰ laird of Woodhouselee, and others, and has been listed since 1979.

The memorial is a Celtic ring cross on an ornamental plinth with a three stepped base, a rough stone foundation and dressed stone above. The principal elevation, to the east, has a large knotwork central boss and surround and smaller knotwork bosses on the upper and lower arms.

There is carved interlocking knotwork on the shaft and an inset coat of arms bearing the motto: "OCCULTUS NON EXTINCTUS" (hidden not extinguished). Above the motto there is an inscription: "To the Glory of God and in loving memory of Christ's departed servants".

The Fraser Tytler Memorial

The former mansion, which was demolished in 1965, stood some 250 metres north-east of the memorial.

The Mansion c 1905
©Midlothian Council Local and Family History Library

To complete the final section of The Way start at the Flotterstone car park (NT232631), walk past the visitor centre and along a good path through trees parallel to the road on the right.

About 200 metres along the path there is a plaque commemorating C T R Wilson who was born at Crosshouse Farm (NT239637) in 1869. Wilson, the son of a sheep farmer graduated in natural science from Cambridge in 1892. He invented the cloud chamber and was awarded the Nobel Prize for physics in 1927. He died at Carlops in 1959.

The path leads on to the metalled road and a little further on go through the gate on the left signed 'Scald Law'. Do not cross Glencorse burn but keep it on your left following the sign for the old filter beds. This area is rich in Pipistrelle bats and you may spot bat roosting boxes. Go through two more gates and past the old filter beds on your left. The track now begins to climb while curving to the right.

At this point it may be worth taking a short detour to view the outfall from Glencorse Reservoir which can be quite dramatic.[12] Where the track begins to climb there is a path to the left which follows the line of Glencorse Burn. Follow the path through trees for about two hundred metres. After viewing the outfall return to the track and follow it up to a wooden gate. At the gate turn left onto the metalled road.

Follow the metalled road north westwards past Glen Cottage on the left and then Glencorse Reservoir. After nearly a kilometre there is a wooden gate on the right, set slightly back from the road, and signed Glencorse View Walk and alongside it a military training area sign with map. Go up the path on the edge of the conifer plantation. At the kissing gate turn left on to a good stony track. Follow this track

Outfall from Glencorse Reservoir

12   The outflow is shut when the reservoir level falls.

which runs north-west and then northwards round the western flank of Castlelaw Hill.

Before turning to the north stop to admire the view over Glencorse Reservoir and to the south-west up the Logan valley towards The Howe with Scald Law and the Kips on the left. The Logan valley is a favourite spot for hearing the first cuckoo in spring and it is also worth looking out for herons and geese.

There are 13 reservoirs of varying sizes in the Pentland Hills most of which were built in the 19th century. Glencorse, Loganlea, Clubbiedean, Torduff and Bonaly were built to supply water to Edinburgh. Threipmuir, Harlaw, Harperrig and Crosswood supplied compensation water for the great number of mills on the Water of Leith although today, with the demise of the mills, their primary use is flood protection. North Esk Reservoir was built by a consortium of Penicuik mill owners to provide power for their mills. Chapter 13 (pp184-198) of *The Call of the Pentlands* has the title *A Ramble Round the Reservoirs* and provides much detail on the construction of the Reservoirs and the bird life which they support.

Glencorse Reservoir was built between 1819 and 1822 and employed a workforce of some 300 men. The Reservoir was designed by Thomas Telford and cost £209,000. It has a capacity of 359,373,000 gallons and a maximum depth of 62 feet. Today Megget and Talla Reservoirs are the main sources of Edinburgh's drinking water; however, Glencorse still provides a top-up supply when necessary and it has inlet points from both Megget and Talla. Glencorse also provides a recreational facility as a fishery. Fishing is by boat only and the Reservoir is stocked with a mix of brown, rainbow and brook trout. Both boat and bank fishing is available at Loganlee Reservoir.

The Logan Valley from Castlelaw

Glencorse Reservoir

Below the waters of the reservoir, just below Kirkton Farm, lies the remains of the chapel of St Katherine in the Hopes and, thereby, hangs a tale. There is a story, related in the *Lay of the Last Minstrel* by Sir Walter Scott, about a Pentland white stag. Robert the Bruce while hunting in the Pentlands found that a white stag always escaped from his hounds. On one occasion he asked his companions if any of them had hounds that could outmatch his. All remained silent except Sir William St Clair of Roslin who wagered his head that his hounds could catch the stag. The King accepted the wager and betted the forest of Pentland against the life of Sir William. Sir William, realising his predicament, prayed to Christ, the Virgin and St Katherine. In answer to his prayers, and at the last moment, one of Sir William's hounds turned the stag and the other killed it. The King embraced Sir William and granted him the lands of Kirkton and Loganhouse. In recognition of his deliverance Sir William built the chapel of St Katherine in the Hopes.[13]

---

13   This story, with a photograph of the ruins, can be found in Pentland Days and Country Ways by Will Grant pp108-115

Stay on the path which climbs steadily keeping the Kirk Burn on the left. After a bit more than a kilometre the path comes to the track from Dreghorn to Castlelaw at NT225658. Go forward over the stile or cattle grid and, with the fence and dry stane wall on your right, climb the ridge to the summit of Allermuir.

Kirkton Farm

Here the panorama surpasses that of Scald Law. On an exceptionally clear day it is sometimes just possible to see the Paps of Jura away to the west and, on most days, the Bass Rock is visible to the east. Beyond the city, the Forth and the Fife coast are the hills of Perthshire. In good visibility you will be able to take time to absorb the full splendour of the view.

Allermuir from the South

View from Summit of Allermuir

The Pentlands' closest association with Edinburgh dates from the period of the Scottish Enlightenment. Henry Cockburn, whose name survives today in Edinburgh's Cockburn Association[14], was born in 1779. He set up his country home at Bonaly when he married in 1811 and he died there in 1854. When Cockburn moved to Bonaly Britain was at war with France to settle the supremacy of British influence in continental Europe and when he died France was Britain's ally in the war against Russia in the Crimea.

Cockburn had a distinguished career at the bar, ultimately becoming a judge. He was also one of the leaders of the Whig party in Scotland and, as Solicitor General, was largely responsible for the Scottish Reform Act of 1832. That Act resulted in the number of voters increasing from under 4,500 to 65,000 – a truly dramatic development.

---

14   See www.cockburnassociation.org.uk

He was also a noted conservationist and a brilliant commentator on events and people. He began to compile private records around 1821 and these formed the basis of works published by his trustees after his death. His most famous work, *Memorials of his Time*, was published in 1856 and remains a work of great interest and academic value. In that work Cockburn tells us that: "There is not a recess in the valleys

Bonaly Tower

of the Pentlands, nor an eminence on their summits, that is not familiar to my solitude".

This was how Cockburn described Edinburgh society in the early 1800s – the second stage of the Scottish Enlightenment.

"The society of Edinburgh had never been better, or indeed so good. It continued in a state of high animation till 1815, or perhaps till 1820. Its brilliancy was owing to a variety of peculiar circumstances which only operated during this period. The principal of these were the survival of several of the eminent men of the preceding age, and of curious old habits which the modern flood had not yet obliterated; the rise of a powerful community of young men of ability; the exclusion of the British from the Continent [because of the Napoleonic wars], which made Edinburgh, both for education and residence, a favourite resort of strangers; the blaze of that popular literature which made Edinburgh the second city in the Empire for learning and science; and the extent and ease with which literature and society embellished each other, without rivalry or pedantry."

Henry Cockburn, Lord Cockburn
by H F (or F H) Weisse, lithograph, 1834 or after
©National Portrait Gallery, London

In Cockburn's day the city extended little beyond the Meadows, but it was growing rapidly. In 1801 the population was less than 100,000 but by 1861 it had risen to over 220,000. Today the city's population is some 490,000.

Cockburn spent much of his early life on the southern edge of the city, just to the south of the Meadows, and he later recalled that: "Under these trees walked, and talked, and meditated, all our literary and scientific, and many of our legal worthies".

Henry Home, Lord Kames, by David Martin
©Scottish National Portrait Gallery

Cockburn was, of course, referring to the major figures of the Scottish Enlightenment. Henry Home, Lord Kames, (1696-1782), by profession a lawyer, but also an agricultural improver, moral philosopher, literary critic and historian. David Hume (1711-1776) the pre-eminent philosopher of his time. Adam Smith (1723-1790), the political economist and author of *The Wealth of Nations.* Adam Ferguson (1723-1816), the philosopher and historian who was present in the ranks at the battle of Fontenoy in 1745 before becoming a member of the ministry. James Hutton (1726-1797), the father of modern geology.

David Hume by Allan Ramsay
©Scottish National Portrait Gallery

Robert Adam (1728-1792), the neo classical architect responsible for Edinburgh's Charlotte Square and Culzean Castle in Ayrshire.

The portrait painters Henry Raeburn (1756-1823), and Allan Ramsay (1773-1850). Of particular note are Raeburn's portraits of Walter Scott in 1822 and the Reverend Robert Walker, the skating minister, in 1790 and Ramsay's portrait of David Hume in 1766.

Sir Walter Scott by Sir Henry Raeburn
©Scottish National Portrait Gallery

These were the 'Men of Letters' that earned Edinburgh the reputation of being a 'hot-bed of genius'. It was their influence that carried the Second Enlightenment into the age of Cockburn, Walter Scott and Cockburn's fellow Whig lawyer, literary critic and lifelong friend Francis Jeffrey.

Michael Fry, writing in *The Scotsman* in the autumn of 2014 tells us that: "The Scottish Enlightenment was an affair of good cheer, good drink, and good talk". He goes on to compare it favourably with "the brittle intellectualism of the French Enlightenment and the idealistic authoritarianism of the German Enlightenment".

Lest we get too carried away with Edinburgh's celebrated intellectual past we should remember the judgement of

Daiches, who extolls the Scottish enlightenment, that: "Late eighteenth century Edinburgh was a city of contrasts: New Town and Old Town; elegance and filth; humanity and cruelty".[15]

Cockburn loved the relationship between Bonaly and the city. He set up the 'Bonaly Friday Club' when Men of Letters joined him in the Pentlands to imbue that relationship. In the autumn of 1853 James Naysmith, of steam hammer fame, was amongst the guests and he left this record of that occasion.

"The day was perfect in all respects. With that most genial of men, Lord Cockburn for our guide, we wandered far up the Pentland Hills. After a rather toilsome walk we reached a favourite spot. We sat down in a semi-circle, our guide in the middle. After settling ourselves to enjoy our well-earned rest we sat in silence for a time. The gentle breeze blew past us and we inhaled the fragrant air. It was enough for a time to look on, for the glorious old city before us, with its towers and spires, and lofty buildings between us and the distance. On one side Arthur's Seat and the other the castle, the crown of the city".

The walker may well imagine that he or she may have been one of Cockburn's guests some 170 years ago and reflect on whether Pentland air and Pentland vistas were a catalyst for the Scottish Enlightenment.

Once again, however, we need to come down from a summit, this time to conclude our journey. Take the obvious path that leads away from the fence and heads down in a north-easterly direction to meet the Swanston to Hillend Ski Centre track at NT238667 with the T-Wood in the background. Continue on the path that leads steeply down towards the hamlet of Swanston.

---

15   Daiches p170

Edinburgh from above Bonaly

ust above Swanston on the left, the walker passes one of he five Pentland arboreta planted by the Friends of the Pentlands in 2013. Immediately opposite the arboretum is he dry stane shelter seat built by the Friends of the Pentlands n memory of their former member, Donald Graham.

The first mention of Swanston dates from 1214 when a farmer called Svienn took out a lease to work the land and, subsequently, gave his name to that land. What we see at Swanston today, however, has its origins in he early 1700s. The quiet, traffic-free, picturesque conservation hamlet nestles around a little stream and contrasts vividly with the burgeoning capital city just a few hundred metres way.

The 'Roaring Shepherd's' Cottage at Swanston

It is an idyllic spot to end The Way, not least because the hamlet is closely associated with one of Scotland's most famous literary figures. John Tod, the 'Roaring Shepherd', whose cottage is pictured above, encouraged Stevenson to love the Pentlands.

Robert Louis Stevenson was born in Howard Place in Edinburgh in 1850. However, his parents leased Swanston Cottage (NT237676) from 1867 to 1880 and, although he travelled widely during those years, and much more widely later in life, Swanston was important to Stevenson and influenced his writing.

Stevenson was the grandson of Robert Stevenson the famous lighthouse engineer. The younger Stevenson read engineering and then law at Edinburgh University, but practised neither, much to the disappointment of his parents.

Swanston Cottage

He was much more interested in following a student's lifestyle than pursuing a conventional career. He wore his hair long and dressed unconventionally. More importantly for someone brought up in a devout Presbyterian household he rejected Christianity, a situation that caused his parents considerable dismay. Stevenson wrote this about his situation. "What a damned curse I am to my parents! As my father said "you have rendered my whole life a failure". As my mother said "This is the heaviest affliction that has ever befallen me". O Lord, what a pleasant thing it is to have damned the happiness of (probably) the only two people who care a damn about you in the world."

By the age of 36 Stevenson is reported to have slept in 50 Scottish towns, 46 in England, 74 in France and 40 in the rest of Europe. Undoubtedly he had a passion for seeing places and people for himself and making his own judgements about the world in which he found himself.

Nevertheless, Edinburgh and its surroundings were central to much of Stevenson's writing. This was how he described the city in the heyday of the Victorian era in 1878.[16]

"Few places, if any, offer a more barbaric display of contrasts to the eye. In the very midst stands one of the most satisfactory crags in nature – a Bass Rock upon dry land, rooted in a garden, shaken by passing trains, carrying a crowd of battlements and turrets, and describing its warlike shadow over the liveliest and brightest thoroughfare of the New Town.

"From their smoky beehives, ten stories high, the unwashed look down upon the open squares and gardens of the wealthy; and gay people sunning themselves along Princes Street, with its mile of commercial palaces all beflagged upon some great occasion, see,

---

16   Quoted in Daiches p210

across a gardened valley set with statues, where the washings of the old town flutter in the breeze at its high windows. And then, upon all sides, what a clashing of architecture! In this one valley, where the life of the town goes most busily forward, there may be seen, shown one above and behind another by the accidents of the ground, buildings in almost every style upon the globe. Egyptian and Greek temples, Venetian palaces and Gothic spires, are huddled one over another in a most admired disorder; while above all, the brute mass of the castle and the summit of Arthur's Seat look down upon these imitations with a becoming dignity."

Stevenson inherited a tendency to coughs and fevers, especially in winter, and illness was a recurrent feature of his adult life and left him unusually thin. In 1880 Stevenson married Fanny Vandegrift Osborne, an American divorcee with three children and ten years his senior. They had first met in France in 1876 while she was still married. For the next seven years Stevenson, who had endured indifferent health since boyhood, searched in vain for a place of residence suitable for his health. Summers were spent largely in Scotland or England and winters in France.

At this time Stevenson was happy with everything but his health and it was during this period that he wrote the bulk of his best known works including *Kidnapped* and *Treasure Island*. In 1888 he chartered a yacht and he and Fanny set out for the south Pacific. After nearly three years of cruising he purchased land on Samoa and settled there.

He continued to write and much of his writing was set in Scotland, such as *The Master of Ballantrae* and *Weir of Hermiston.* "It is a singular thing", he wrote, "that I should live here in the South Seas, under conditions so new and so striking, and yet my imagination so continually inhabits the cold old huddle of grey hill from which we came."

Robert Louis Stevenson by
Count Girolamo Nerli ©Scottish National Portrait Gallery

And, from Samoa he wrote:

> "The tropics vanish; and meseems that I –
> from Halkerside, from topmost Allermuir,
> or steep Caerketton – dreaming, gaze again."

e had long feared a lingering death; however, he died suddenly in
amoa in 1894, probably of a cerebral haemorrhage, at the age of 44.

he Way ends at Swanston where, if the plan is to continue by bus,
e walker can head north down the road and over the city by-pass to
xgangs Road or, alternatively, to head east on the well-marked path to
othianburn on the A702.

However, if sustenance is required the Swanston Golf Club is open to non-golfers and offers a range of food and drink. A short stop here to reflect on The Way and sample some Pentland produce makes a fitting ending to the journey.

For details visit: www.swanstonbrasserie.co.uk

Swanston Brasserie

Although Swanston now provides a range of recreational facilities it is still a working farm with a variety of livestock in the fields and on the hill.

Highland Cow above Swanston

The summit of Mendick Hill

Kirkton Cottage and Glencorse

REFLECTIONS

Your walk with history is now complete. Having enjoyed the physical exercise and admired the varied and often exceptional views remember what lies beneath the surface.

Take time to reflect on the richness of our heritage and remember, with humility and admiration, those who trod these paths before us and unwittingly made our experience so enlightening and rewarding. Reflect also on those who live and work in the Pentlands today. They understand and appreciate our heritage and, like the Friends of the Pentlands, seek to conserve, protect and enhance our environment. Protecting the past does not, and should not, conflict with sensible progress, not least because change is inevitable. Look back with appreciation, but look forward with enthusiasm.

Pentland Inspiration

Walter Scott rented a cottage in Lasswade from 1798 to 1804. During that period he knew the Pentlands well and left us this memory: "I think I never saw anything more beautiful than the ridge of Carnethy against a clear frosty sky."

The Pentlands are not Scotland's most spectacular hills, but they are probably its most intriguing, steeped as they are in our rich cultural past. Today the 'Call of the Pentlands' is every bit as strong as it was when Will Grant wrote his charming book about 'our' hills a century ago. Respond to that vibrant call.

A final thought.

> "Breathes there the man, with soul so dead,
> Who never to himself hath said,
> This is my own, my native land!
> Whose heart hath ne'er within him burned,
> As home his footsteps he hath turned
> From wandering on a foreign strand!

The Lay of the Last Minstrel (1805) by Sir Walter Scott

IN PENTLAND WINE
By Will H Ogilvie

Up here with the wind in our faces,
And the brown heath under our feet,
We look through the shimmering spaces
Over tower and steeple and street
To the lion splendidly sleeping,
To the tall crags silent and grey
To the Castle its grim guard keeping,
And the shining shield of the Bay.

Behind us the mist of the valley
Lie low on the moorland's breast,
With the bonnie banks of Bonaly
In the grey of the winter dressed.
The west wind, wanton, is chiding
Glencorse with the scourge of his whips,
And the wild ducks over it riding
Are tossing like storm-tossed ships.

Up here with the clear winds blowing,
I look to you, City of mine,
I fill me a goblet o'erflowing
And pledge you in Pentland wine!
With a full heart thrilled by your story,
While the hills stand round like kings,
I drink to your lasting glory
In the wine that the hill-wind brings!

Quoted, with much appreciation, from Pentland Walks, edited by Robert
Cochrane, Andrew Elliot, Edinburgh, 1908

BIBLIOGRAPHY

Anderson, Rab, *The Pentland Hills,* Mica Publishing, Glasgow and Edinburgh, 2011

Anderson, W, *The Pentland Hills,* W & R Chambers, Edinburgh, 1926

Baldwin, J R, *Exploring Scotland's Heritage, Edinburgh, Lothians and Borders,* RCAHMS, The Stationery Office, 1997

Baldwin, John and Drummond, Peter, *Pentland Place Names: An Introductory Guide,* Friends of the Pentlands, Meigle Colour Printers, Tweedbank, Galashields, 2011

Bogle, Kenneth & Falconer, Susan, *The Pentland Hills,* Stenlake Publishing Ltd, 2010

Cochrane, Robert, *Pentland Walks with their Literary and Historical Associations,* Andrew Elliot, Edinburgh, 1918

Crumley, J, *Discovering the Pentland Hills,* John Donald, 1991

Daiches, David, *Edinburgh,* Hamish Hamilton, London, 1978

Falconer, Susan, *The Pentland Hills: A Walker's Guide,* Cicerone, Milnthrope, Cumbria, 2007

Friends of the Pentlands: *Something for Everyone,* Meigle Colour Printers, Tweedbank, Galashields

Friends of the Pentlands, *Woodhouselee and the Fraser Tytler Family,* 2012

Gordon, J E, and Sutherland, D G, (eds), *Quaternary of Scotland,* Chapman and Hall, 1993

Grant, Will, *The Call of the Pentlands,* Oliver and Boyd, Edinburgh, 1927

Grant, Will, *Pentland Days and Country Ways*, Thomas Nelson and Sons Ltd, Edinburgh, 1934

Lawson, J, and Truman, M, *A Shepherd's Life,* Scottish National Portrait Gallery, 2000

Reith, G M, *The Breezy Pentlands,* T N Foulis, 1910

ScotWays, *The Pentland Hills: Their Paths and Passes,* Macniven & Wallace, Edinburgh, 1904

INDEX